MIND OF
A CRIMINAL

# MIND OF
# A CRIMINAL

ODYSSEYS

VALERIE BODDEN

CREATIVE EDUCATION · CREATIVE PAPERBACKS

Published by Creative Education and Creative Paperbacks
P.O. Box 227, Mankato, Minnesota 56002
Creative Education and Creative Paperbacks
are imprints of The Creative Company
www.thecreativecompany.us

Design by Blue Design (www.bluedes.com)
Production by Joe Kahnke
Art direction by Rita Marshall
Printed in China

Photographs by Alamy (AF archive, Collection Christophel,
ZUMA Press Inc.), AP Images (LENNOX MCLENDON/
Associated Press), Creative Commons Wikimedia (U.S.
National Archives and Records Administration/Ronald Reagan
Presidential Library), Getty Images (Bettmann, Chicago
Tribune, Bill Frakes, Ed Lallo, New York Daily News Archive,
Past Pix), iStockphoto (Yuri_Arcurs, bajker, Sproetniek,
P_Wei), Mary Evans Picture Library, Newscom (POOL-Elaine
Thompson/ZUMAPRESS), Shutterstock (Maryna Babych,
Carlos Caetano, Levent Konuk, luxorphoto, Jaroslav Monchak)

Library of Congress Cataloging-in-Publication Data
Names: Bodden, Valerie, author.
Title: Mind of a criminal / Valerie Bodden.
Series: Odysseys in crime scene science.
Includes bibliographical references and index.
Summary: An in-depth look at how psychological profilers
analyze behaviors and patterns to identify suspects and help
solve crimes, employing real-life examples such as the Jeffrey
Dahmer case.
Identifiers: LCCN 2015027748 / ISBN 978-1-60818-684-6
(hardcover) / ISBN 978-1-62832-473-0 (pbk) / ISBN 978-1-
56660-720-9 (eBook)

Subjects: LCSH: 1. Criminal behavior, Prediction of—Juvenile
literature. 2. Criminal investigation—Juvenile literature.
3. Criminal psychology—Juvenile literature. 4. Forensic
psychology—Juvenile literature.
Classification: LCC HV6027.B63 2016 / DDC 363.25—dc23

CCSS: RI 8.1, 2, 3, 4, 5, 8, 10; RI 9-10.1, 2, 3, 4, 5, 8, 10; RI 11-12.1, 2,
3, 4, 5, 10; RST 6-8.1, 2, 5, 6, 10; RST 9-10.1, 2, 5, 6, 10; RST 11-12.1,
2, 5, 6, 10

First Edition HC 9 8 7 6 5 4 3 2 1
First Edition PBK 9 8 7 6 5 4 3 2 1

# CONTENTS

# Introduction

Blue and red lights sweep across the front of a home. They reflect off jagged shards of glass in a broken first-floor window. Inside, books and pictures have been tossed to the floor. Papers hang from ransacked drawers. Two plates—their food still warm—sit on the kitchen table. A small red spot stains the floor under one of the chairs. This looks like a crime scene. But by the time police

**OPPOSITE:** When someone places a distress call to an emergency dispatcher, the dispatcher will immediately notify and direct first responders—including police officers, firemen, or emergency medical technicians—to the location. First responders provide aid to those at the scene.

arrived, the house was empty. Now investigators must use crime scene science to help solve the mystery of what happened here—and who did it.

Crime scene science is also referred to as forensic science. Forensic science is simply science that is used to solve crimes and provide facts in a legal trial. Solving a crime often involves many forensic scientists, each specializing in a different area. In a case where the police have a hard time identifying suspects or a **motive**, forensic **psychologists** might be called in to help. These forensic experts put together a profile of the type of person who might have committed the crime. Their analysis might just be the clue that leads police to the perpetrator.

# Personality of a Perpetrator

Are you quiet and shy or loud and outgoing? Do you prefer hugs or handshakes? A walk in the woods or a sprint down the football field? All of our values, attitudes, and preferences combine to form our personality. Each person has a unique personality shaped by biology, culture, surroundings, and experiences.

Psychology is the study of the mind, emotions, and behavior. Forensic psychology applies that study to the law. It hinges on understanding the personality of criminals. According to psychologist Dr. Stanton Samenow, "We must understand how criminals think and realize that they have a fundamentally different view of the world from that of people who are basically responsible."

Psychologists have discovered that our behaviors reflect our personality. Forensic psychologists hold that what a criminal does at a crime scene also shows his or her personality. By analyzing that behavior, they hope to learn enough about the personality of the person who committed the crime to create a profile. This is a list of features that can help law enforcement identify a specific suspect.

The job of a profiler is to look at a crime and draw conclusions about the person who committed it. The Federal Bureau of Investigation (FBI) calls profiling "behavioral analysis." It stresses that such analysis "is all about better understanding criminals and terrorists—who they are, how they think, why they do what they do—as a means to help solve crimes and prevent attacks."

For the majority of crimes, profiling is not necessary. In many cases, the motive for a crime is obvious. Missing cash or valuables can indicate greed or a need for money. A husband who finds his wife cheating on him may kill out of jealousy. In such instances, the police are often easily able to develop a list of suspects.

But when police officers cannot pinpoint a motive or suspect, they might call on a profiler. This is especially true in cases of serial crimes such as murder, rape, arson, or robbery. In the case of a kidnapping, where time is an important factor, profilers may be called in to help guide the search.

According to the FBI, serial killers are murderers who kill at least two victims (and often many more) in separate events. There is a "cooling-off period," or break, between the murders. The FBI puts the number of at-large serial killers in the United States at any given time between 25 and 50. Profilers such as Pat Brown think that number is much higher. Brown

# FAMOUS CRIMES

POLICE · BUDGET · EDITION    EDITED · BY · HAROLD · FURNISS

PAST · AND · PRESENT    ONE · PENNY

THE DISCOVERY OF "JACK THE RIPPER'S" FIRST MURDER.

# Jack the Ripper

In 1888, a serial killer terrorized London, killing at least five women. The killer soon became known as Jack the Ripper. Britain's first profiler, Dr. Thomas Bond, analyzed the killer. He believed Jack the Ripper would be a man of "great coolness and daring." He would be quiet and neat but strange and unstable. In addition, he probably had surgical experience. Sir Arthur Conan Doyle, who had published the first Sherlock Holmes story a year earlier, entered his opinion, too. He thought the killer was a woman—probably a nurse. Over the years, numerous names have been put forward as suspects, including Prince Edward Albert, the grandson of Queen Victoria. But the killer was never identified. The Jack the Ripper story lives on in numerous movies, TV shows, and books today.

estimates that there could be as many as 40 serial killers in each state. That makes a total of 2,000 serial killers in the country. But, Brown emphasizes, "These are not all active at the same time, so over a decade, some may do little and some may be very busy."

Cases of serial murder are often particularly gruesome. Bodies may show evidence of torture. The killer may commit the murder with his own hands, such as by strangling or stabbing. There might also be signs of overkill. For example, the killer might stab a person many times, even after the victim is dead. Such evidence can indicate to profilers that the killer is a **psychopath**. In general, psychopaths do not care about others. They are incapable of feeling sorry for what they've done.

Serial killers can be particularly difficult to catch. For one thing, their motive is often unclear to investigators. Some may kill simply for fame, revenge, or lust. Others kill for excitement. They want "the high voltage of doing what is forbidden, illegal, something that others would not dare to do or even think of doing," according to Samenow. "As one man said, 'Crime is delicious; it's like ice cream.' Another commented, 'Take my crime away, and you take my world away.'"

Serial killers are also hard to find because they often live double lives. The people who know them are often shocked to learn what they have done. Robert Yates, for example, was a decorated helicopter pilot with the U.S. Army National Guard. He lived in Spokane, Washington, with his wife and five children. No one was aware that throughout the 1990s, Yates was responsible for killing 16 women. He even buried one of them in his yard.

Serial murder investigations can go on for years. At first, the murders may not be recognized as serial crimes, especially if they occur in different areas. Once it becomes clear that police are dealing with a serial offender, though, a profiler is often called in. The profiler uses crime scene photos, autopsy reports, lab reports, and witness statements. She considers how, when, and where the crime was committed. She takes time to learn about the victim. The profiler also looks at statistical information about similar crimes and their offenders. For most profilers, gut feeling plays a role as well. Former FBI behavioral analyst John Douglas said that after considering all the evidence, he would "put myself mentally and emotionally in the head of the offender."

Ultimately, the profiler tries to come up with a reasonable estimation of the offender's personality. Is he a loner or married, paranoid or trusting, aggressive or withdrawn? The profiler also tries to determine other features such as age, race, gender, job, and education. She even tries to figure out where the perpetrator lives. Police can then use the profile to narrow down a list of suspects. Once they have a suspect in custody, the profile can help police figure out how best to question him. In some cases, the profile might also give clues about the likely timing and location of the next attack. For example, in one case, a serial killer had murdered four women in four months. Profilers were able to predict the exact date of the next attack. As a result, the police caught the killer.

# Examining the Evidence

Analysts use inductive and deductive profiling to develop a picture of a suspect. Inductive profiling assumes that those who commit a certain type of crime have similar backgrounds, personalities, and motives. According to criminal profiling experts Ronald Holmes and Stephen Holmes, "It would be a mistake to say that all serial killers think alike." But, they say, "It would also be foolhardy to assume that there are not some similarities among them."

This type of profiling uses statistics to define the "typical" person involved in a certain crime. For example, 88 percent of all serial killers are male. About 85 percent are white. Their average age is 28.5 years at the time of their first murder. Many serial killers were abused as children. They may have a criminal history of committing more serious crimes over time. Some are also highly interested in police work. They may even spend their time around police officers or active crime scenes. Serial killer Jeffrey Dahmer murdered 17 young men and kept parts of their bodies in his freezer. Although police did not develop a profile on Dahmer, he would have fit the profile of the typical serial killer perfectly. He was 31 years old, white, and male. Like many serial killers, he was also charming and a loner. And he worked an unskilled job despite being very smart.

Of course, there are exceptions. Wayne Williams, also known as the Atlanta Child Killer, was black. So was Derrick Todd Lee, who killed at least six women in Baton Rouge, Louisiana. Charles Ng, from China, killed many victims in California. And Angel Maturino Resendiz, from Mexico, killed more than nine people across the U.S. Women, too, have been serial killers. Aileen Wuornos killed seven men in Florida.

## Historical Profile

In the 1800s, many people believed that certain physical signs could be used to recognize people who were born to be criminals. These features included a large jaw or cheekbones, long arms, or ears that were smaller or larger than average. But in 1888, Dr. Thomas Bond of Britain created the first criminal profile based on behavior. Ten years later, Austrian judge Hans Gross published *Criminal Psychology*. The book explored the psychological aspects of crime. In the 1950s, **psychiatrist** James Brussel created an accurate profile of a serial bomber in New York. The FBI opened its Behavioral Science Unit in 1972. In 2001, the American Psychological Association made forensic psychology an approved specialty in the field.

And Dorothea Puente killed nine elderly and mentally disabled tenants of her California boarding house.

Such exceptions mean that inductive profiling is not always accurate. "The reality is that criminal behavior, like all human behavior, is complex, and there is no 'one-size-fits-all' profile for any type of offender," said former FBI behavioral analyst Gregg McCrary. "When I'm asked, 'What is the profile of a [serial murderer]?' I reply, 'There is none,' because even for similar types of predators, we have no formula. They remain individuals."

That is where deductive profiling comes in. Such profiles are based on the evidence found at a particular crime scene. The profiler tries to determine the offender's characteristics and personality according to his behavior there. Helpful clues may consist of the weapon used or the position of the body. Even a footprint can be useful. It can indicate the culprit's size. But, more than that, it can reveal whether he was walking, running, or pacing. All of this can point to his mental state. How a killer captures his victims can also have meaning. From 1979 to 1981, the Trailside Killer murdered seven hikers in the San Francisco area. Profiler John Douglas concluded that the killer was white, in his 30s, smart, and shy. He also reasoned that the killer had a speech impediment. That is why he attacked his victims in secluded places.

He would not have been able to talk them into going anywhere with him. David Carpenter was arrested as the Trailside Killer in 1981. Although Carpenter was in his 50s, not 30s, police were stunned that Douglas had been right about his severe stutter.

As they examine the crime scene, profilers also try to identify the criminal's method of operating. This refers to the way the offender commits the crime. It can include how he enters a home, what he steals, the time he strikes, what he wears, or the weapons he uses. Evidence of a pattern can help investigators link crimes committed by the same person. But the pattern might change over time. The criminal might learn new methods or try to avoid being caught.

n the case of serial crimes, the offender also often leaves a signature. This is his way of "signing" the work. In late-1800s London, for example, serial killer Jack the Ripper's signature was the partial dissection of his victims. More recently, the Texas Eyeball Killer removed the eyeballs of his victims. A signature doesn't have to be gruesome. The killer may also leave a note

or other object. In some cases, the position of the body serves as a signature. In addition to helping investigators link crimes, a signature can show them what the serial killer is thinking. "Signatures [are] a clue not only to what the murderer does, but what he wants, what he seeks, and what drives him from victim to victim," according to former detective Robert Keppel. "Signatures are the only ways the killer truly expresses himself."

any profilers divide serial killers into two categories: organized or disorganized. An organized

"Signatures [are] a clue not only to what the murderer does, but what he wants, what he seeks, and what drives him from victim to victim."

serial killer has a careful plan in place before committing his crime. He is often smart and charming. He may even have a family and a good job. An organized serial killer is likely to dispose of the body somewhere separate from the murder scene. Ted Bundy, a college graduate and law student, for example, disposed of most of his 30 victims in heavily wooded areas. The organized killer also cleans up evidence. He removes the weapon from the scene. But during the investigation, he might return to the scene. He might even volunteer tips to the police. Often, tricking the police becomes a game.

The disorganized offender often has no plan. Or he might forget his plan when he begins to commit the crime. These killers might have below-average intelligence. Sometimes they stand out to others as strange. Most live alone and are unwilling to travel far from home. Because their attacks aren't generally planned, disorganized offenders may not carry a weapon. Instead, they will use whatever they find at the scene. They might even leave the weapon behind! Disorganized offenders also tend to leave other evidence, including blood, footprints, and the victim's body. Most offenders fall somewhere between organized and disorganized. A killer might bring a weapon to the scene, for example, but then panic and fail to clean up some of the evidence.

# Digging Deeper

In addition to learning about the kind of person a serial killer is, authorities need to know where they will most likely find him. To figure this out, they might conduct a geographic profile. This type of profile takes into account all the locations associated with a serial killer's crimes. It logs where the offender first made contact with the victim, where the crime was committed, and where the body was found.

**OPPOSITE:** Serial killers are believed to be responsible for less than 1 percent of the 15,000 murders committed every year in the U.S. That adds up to about 150 victims a year. Serial murders have been gradually declining since the 1980s.

By mapping these sites for all the crimes associated with a particular killer, the profiler might be able to figure out the killer's location. Most serial killers are geographically stable. That is, they commit their crimes near where they live. John Wayne Gacy committed all 33 of his murders inside his Chicago home, for example. He buried most of his victims there as well.

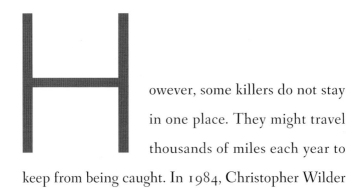owever, some killers do not stay in one place. They might travel thousands of miles each year to keep from being caught. In 1984, Christopher Wilder

**BELOW** As police questioned John Wayne Gacy about a missing teenager, they noticed a foul smell in the house. They discovered 29 bodies in the crawl space of Gacy's home. Four more victims were found in a nearby river. Gacy was sentenced to death in 1980.

killed eight women in six weeks. His cross-country spree ended with his death in New Hampshire. Afterward, he became a leading suspect in two earlier murders even farther away—in Australia.

Today, most geographic profiling is carried out using computer programs. These programs determine the distance from the various crime scenes to different points on the map. The program then assigns probabilities that the killer lives in a specific area. Once a potential location has been identified, investigators start watching the area. They might interview local residents, too. In 1999, investigators in Spokane, Washington, used geographical profiling to plot the locations of several dead women found with bags over their heads. They also plotted the locations of the stores from which the bags had come. The profile led them to the South Hill neighborhood of

Spokane. Eventually, police identified Robert Yates as their serial killer. They discovered that the geographical profile had been right. Yates lived in South Hill.

Geographical profiling can be used for other crimes, such as burglary, as well. In the early 2000s, a burglar in Irvine, California, robbed more than 200 homes. In 2005, a computerized geographic profile predicted both where the burglar might live and where he might strike next. Police set up operations near the likely targets. They soon arrested the burglar, who had

thousands of stolen goods in his home.

In addition to analyzing *where* an offender strikes, profilers can learn a lot from *whom* he strikes. Creating a profile of the victims of a serial killer is known as victimology. According to Holmes and Holmes, "The more one knows about the victim, the more one knows about the offender."

Victimology includes information on the victim's appearance, habits, friends, education, job, and lifestyle. It can help profilers figure out why the killer chose particular victims. Generally, serial killers attack strangers. They usually don't know anything about the person. To a serial killer, the person is "nothing more than a mere object ... to be seized and used as he sees fit," according to Holmes and Holmes.

Even so, many serial killers develop a pattern of

going after certain types of victims. Sometimes they do so **subconsciously**. "If I had made a composite of my 'typical' victim, it would read like this: The individual would be white, female, between the ages of 13 and 19," said one serial killer. "It was not entirely conscious.... I was roaming the streets in search of females in general, but with no specific age group in mind. Yet 75 percent of the time the person who 'clicked' and 'registered' in my mind was the girl I described above." Often, the ideal victim represents someone who has hurt or rejected the killer in the past. The victim might remind the killer of his mother, for example. Or she might look like the girls who laughed at him in high school. According to Holmes and Holmes, even though serial killers often have an "ideal" victim in mind, their actual victim may not always fit the pattern. This could be because it's easier to grab someone else. Or, the killer might grow impatient and feel the need to kill immediately.

Patterns such as victim types, methods, and signatures are often key to identifying serial killers. But these can be hard to identify if the killer operates in a wider geographical area or spreads out his crimes over time. That is why such patterns are tracked using various databases, including the FBI's Violent Criminal Apprehension Program (ViCAP). This program catalogs up to 100 features from each crime to identify similarities. ViCAP has had some notable successes. In 1999, the program connected serial killer Angel Maturino Resendiz with several murders. Those murders were committed along railroad lines in Kentucky, Illinois, and Texas. Authorities believe Resendiz may have killed people in Florida, California, and Georgia as well.

## Profiling Hitler

In 1943, the U.S. Office of Strategic Services needed a profile of German leader Adolf Hitler. They wanted to know what Hitler might do if Germany were defeated in World War II. Psychiatrist Walter Langer was asked to develop the profile. Langer noted that Hitler had been influenced by his cold, abusive father and overly affectionate mother. He said Hitler was unable to form strong relationships. Langer's profile also reported that Hitler loved classical music and circus acts that put people in danger. He feared germs and moonlight. And he always crossed a room diagonally from one corner to another while whistling a marching tune. Based on this profile, Langer concluded that if Germany were defeated, Hitler would most likely commit suicide. He turned out to be right.

A criminal profile is never considered complete. As the investigation continues, profilers might uncover facts that give additional insight into the offender's character. Investigators use these facts to help them question suspects. An organized killer generally needs to be confronted directly and with confidence, for example. The questioner can show no signs of doubt or weakness. When interviewing a disorganized offender, though, the officer may need to act friendly to gain the offender's trust. Accusations should be made indirectly.

In addition to being questioned, suspects may be asked to take a polygraph test. Although this device is often referred to as a lie detector, it cannot tell whether a person is lying. Instead, it measures the body's response to stress. Stress can indicate that a person is lying. A

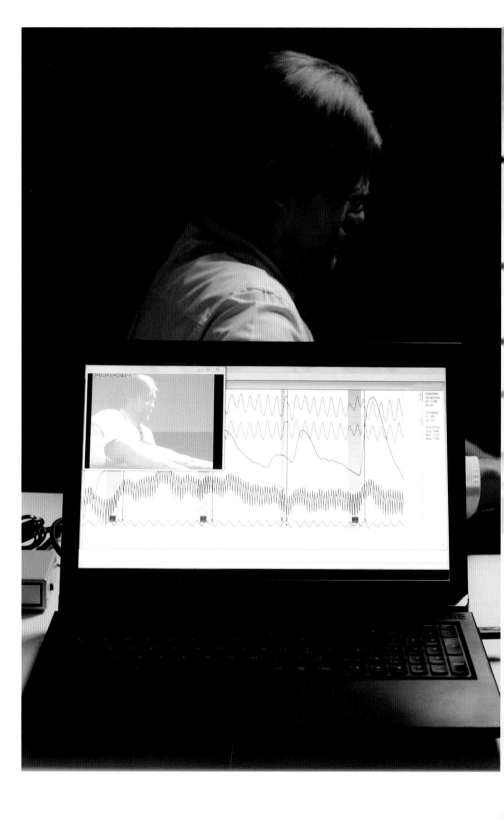

polygraph monitors a person's pulse and blood pressure and rate and depth of breathing. It also records changes in the electrical resistance of skin (because sweating increases skin's ability to conduct electricity). The results of these measurements are graphed on a computer screen or printed on paper. In most cases, polygraph results are not allowed in court. But they can help police tighten a suspect pool by ruling out those who pass the test. Sometimes, the threat of a polygraph is enough to make people confess.

# Profiles in Fiction

Forensic psychology has played a role in works of fiction since 1841. That's when the first detective story, Edgar Allan Poe's "The Murders in the Rue Morgue," was published. In the story, detective C. Auguste Dupin has to solve the murder of an old woman and her daughter. He creates a profile of the killer that leads him right to the culprit—an escaped orangutan.

Dupin paved the way for a fictional detective who would become even more famous: Sherlock Holmes. The creation of Scottish author Sir Arthur Conan Doyle, Holmes was based largely on Dr. Joseph Bell, a medical professor of Doyle's. Bell was known for his ability to accurately profile a stranger based solely on observation. Doyle gave this same ability to his fictional detective. Holmes could look at a person's shirtsleeve and tell his education, occupation, residence, and even history. In *The Sign of Four* (1890), Holmes deduces the killer's psychological state based on footprints left at the scene. In "The Boscombe Valley Mystery" (1891), he determines that the attacker is left-handed and walks with a limp. And in *A Study in Scarlet* (1887), he interprets clues at the scene to figure out that the killer's motive was personal, not political. He also determines the killer's height, nationality, and even the length of his fingernails.

The role of profiling in fiction has only become more popular in recent decades. The trend was sparked by Thomas Harris's bestselling thrillers *Red Dragon* (1981) and *The Silence of the Lambs* (1988). *Red Dragon* follows profiler Will Graham. Graham has to catch "The Tooth Fairy," a serial killer who strikes during full moons. Throughout the novel, Graham relies on the insights of former serial killer Hannibal Lecter. In *The Silence of the Lambs*, young agent-in-training Clarice Starling has to interview Lecter as the FBI tries to catch yet another serial killer. In both books, former psychiatrist Lecter proves to be the best profiler. He knows the mind of serial killers from the inside.

Another famed fictional profiler is James Patterson's Alex Cross, who appears in more than 20 novels. The

movies *Kiss the Girls* (1997), *Along Came a Spider* (2001), and *Alex Cross* (2012) are loosely based on the books. Cross is an FBI agent with a doctorate in psychology. He uses his profiling skills in almost every case. In *Roses Are Red* (2000), for example, Cross creates a profile of a bank robber who is also a murderer. "He's a white male between 35 and 50. He's probably well-educated, with a thorough knowledge of banks and their security systems. He may have worked for a financial institution in the past, ... and might have a grudge against them. He robs banks for the money, but the murders are probably for revenge."

Forensic psychology has also played a leading role in a number of television dramas. Perhaps the best-known crime show in recent years is *CSI: Crime Scene Investigation* and its spinoffs. Investigators on these shows create profiles, analyze psychopaths, and develop interrogation strategies. Many episodes feature serial killers who are identified by their method or signature. For example, one serial killer leaves a strand of hair, along with notes and artwork, at his crime scenes. On *Motive*, detective Angie Flynn works to identify what drives the killer in each case. Although she is not a psychologist, "she has the ability to see into that dark place where the motivation to kill is born," according to ABC.com. Behavioral study also plays a prominent role on *Law & Order: SVU*. On that show, forensic psychiatrist George Huang uses his expertise to create profiles of violent criminals. Based on real-life cases, *Criminal Minds* features a group of elite agents from the FBI's Behavioral Analysis Unit. Whenever a serial killer strikes, team members head to the scene to create a profile. In most cases, the profile is the key to solving the case.

Although many crime shows feature storylines taken right from the headlines, they are not always accurate in their portrayal of crime scene science. For one thing, a psychological analysis takes

Because of their inaccuracies, fictional accounts may mislead viewers as to what psychological profiling can do.

much longer than shown on TV. Criminal investigator Guy Antinozzi and author Alan Axelrod mocked the ability of TV profilers to come up with an instant profile. "They arrive at a crime scene, slip on the latex gloves, pick up a few pieces of evidence, stand back and survey the scene, frown, grimace, then raise their eyebrows and declare, 'The doer is a white guy, early twenties, brown hair, brown eyes, and a fan of *Seinfeld* reruns. Let's go get him!'" In reality, it can take days or weeks of poring over documents and conducting interviews to create a criminal profile. Even then, a profile is only one part of an investigation. It must be combined with other evidence in order to catch and convict a killer. Although fictional profilers are almost never wrong, real-life profiling is not an exact science. Profiles are open to a great deal of interpretation. In addition, fictional forensic psychologists are often chased by killers or do battle with the bad guys. But, in reality, these people rarely go into the field. Most of their work is done behind a desk.

Because of their inaccuracies, fictional accounts may mislead viewers as to what psychological profiling can do.

Some worry that it can also give killers ideas on how to avoid getting caught. For example, serial killer Edmund Kemper was tempted to return to the scene of his crimes. But he resisted because he had "seen one too many stories of one too many people" who had been caught that way. Other killers have tried to trick investigators by altering their crime scenes to mislead profilers. Gary Ridgway, also known as the Green River Killer, left gum and cigarette butts at his crime scenes. But he neither chewed gum nor smoked.

# You Be the Profiler

You can learn a lot about a person from their behavior and likes. Ask 10 people to make a list of their favorite activities and foods. Have them write down the kinds of clothes they wear, too. They should not put their name or age on the paper. When they are done, collect all the papers. Look at each to see what you can tell about the person's age and personality based on the information included. For example, maybe someone wrote that they like to skateboard and play basketball, wear athletic shorts, and eat pizza. You might conclude that this person is a 13- to 18-year-old male. He might be athletic and outgoing. Can you match each description to the person who wrote it?

# To Profile or Not to Profile?

Forensic psychology involves more than just profiling. Specialists are also often called on to determine whether a defendant is mentally **competent** to stand trial. A person may be ruled incompetent if she has a mental disorder that prevents her from understanding and participating in the trial. Once a psychologist determines that mental competence has been restored (such as through medication), the trial proceeds.

**OPPOSITE:** A 2006 survey found that 40 percent of forensic psychologists and psychiatrists believe criminal profiling is scientifically valid. This was largely thanks to a significant amount of criminal profiling being done by trained law enforcement officials rather than mental health professionals.

Psychologists are also called on when the defendant pleads not guilty by reason of insanity. The insanity defense considers the defendant's mental condition at the time the crime was committed. In the U.S., the definition of "insanity" varies from state to state. In some states, the defendant is declared insane if she can prove she did not know right from wrong at the time of the crime. Those declared insane are not held legally responsible for their crimes. But the insanity defense doesn't always work. John Wayne Gacy, for example, pleaded insanity. He said he had such a strong impulse to murder that he couldn't help himself. But he was convicted after prosecutors showed he had planned his murders ahead of time.

Forensic psychologists are often called to testify in criminal trials. During the sentencing phase of a trial, they might make treatment suggestions. Or they might

In 1981, John W. Hinckley Jr. attempted to assassinate president Ronald Reagan. Found not guilty by reason of insanity, Hinckley was committed to a psychiatric hospital. In 2016, a federal judge declared he was no longer a threat, and Hinckley was released.

be asked to predict whether the offender will likely commit future crimes. Sometimes they also testify at parole hearings. Their information about the offender's behavior, mental state, and likelihood to reenter criminal activity can influence whether the prisoner is released.

Many profilers begin their careers in law enforcement. They may or may not have a degree in psychology. They receive additional on-the-job training in behavioral science. Large police departments may employ their own profilers. The FBI has an entire Behavioral

Analysis Unit made up of agents specialized in profiling. In order to get a position in that unit, an agent must have a four-year degree and at least three years' experience in the FBI. He or she must also take a 16-week training course on forensic psychology.

Outside law enforcement, forensic psychologists work in prisons, psychiatric hospitals, law firms, or private practices. They may occasionally be consulted by police departments to create a criminal profile. More often, they evaluate an offender's mental state after he has been arrested. They determine competence and may also provide psychological treatment. Forensic psychologists can spend up to 12 years earning a doctorate. Afterward, they enroll in additional specialized training. Forensic psychiatrists carry out many of the same roles as forensic psychologists. They evaluate for competence and treat mentally ill offenders. Sometimes they create profiles. Forensic psychiatrists hold a medical degree rather than a doctorate.

F orensic psychologists and psychiatrists face many challenges. On a daily basis, they witness gruesome and violent acts. They also regularly work with mentally ill and often violent patients. Through it all, they must remain objective. They cannot let their personal feelings cloud their judgment of the person's mental state. However, there is no way for anyone to know for certain what is going on in another's mind. Profiling is subject to interpretation. As former FBI agent McCrary pointed out, "Not everyone will interpret the clues in the same manner."

In some cases, profilers have been flat-out wrong. In 2002, for example, a sniper killed nine people in Washington, D.C. Profilers said the sniper was a lone white man who was smart and had no children. But "the sniper" turned out to be two black males. One was 41 years old and had four children. The other was 17. Neither was particularly smart.

Some experts argue that even when a profile appears to be spot on, it's because many profiles are so vague that they could apply to almost anyone. In addition, there is no way to verify much of the information included in many profiles. Plus, when a suspect is caught, investigators may emphasize those parts of the profile that match.

# Psychological Insight or Party Trick?

In the 1940s and '50s, the Mad Bomber planted more than 30 bombs in New York City. Psychiatrist James Brussel created a profile of the culprit. He estimated the bomber was in his 40s, neat, and foreign. He also predicted the bomber would be wearing a double-breasted suit when he was caught—and he was right. Brussel's accuracy gave new credibility to profiling. But modern critics think it may have been a trick. "Brussel did not really understand the mind of the Mad Bomber," says journalist Malcolm Gladwell. "He seems to have understood only that, if you make a great number of predictions, the ones that were wrong will soon be forgotten." Literary scholar Donald Foster agrees. He says that most of Brussel's predictions, such as the suspect's age and appearance, were incorrect.

Meanwhile, areas that don't line up may be ignored.

Profiling is still considered a relatively new forensic science. Profilers are always looking for ways to make their predictions more accurate. Forensic psychologist Richard Kocsis thinks that profilers have to go back to the beginning and define what a forensic profile even is. "What types of information do, or should, profiles contain?" he asks. "What type of case material do you need to construct a profile?" Kocsis and others also believe profiling needs to become more scientific and research-based.

Other scientists have worked to make lie detection more scientific. A new procedure called brain finger-printing involves showing a subject a series of words and images. As the person looks at the pictures, scientists monitor her brainwaves. Whenever she sees an image she recognizes, it triggers a change in certain brainwaves. If the subject's brainwaves react to an image of something from the crime scene, it signals that this information is already stored in her memory. "These are details the subject would have no reason [to know] unless he committed the crime—that's solid evidence," said **neuroscientist** Lawrence Farwell. Researchers are also looking for ways to use **magnetic resonance imaging** (MRI) scans and **voice stress analysis** to detect lies.

Even with these new advances, forensic psychology is never likely to be a foolproof science. That's because it is based on interpretations of human nature. Profilers cannot use scientific tests to come up with a profile perfectly matched to one person. Instead, they rely on educated guesses. As Holmes and Holmes stress, profiling "is only one tool and by itself has never solved a murder

case." Even so, a criminal profile can give police a place to start their investigation. And forensic psychologists can help determine what should happen to offenders after their arrest. With researchers digging ever deeper into the minds of criminals, forensic psychology is likely to remain an important part of crime scene science well into the future.

# Glossary

**autopsy**     a medical examination performed on a dead body to determine the cause of death

**competent**     having the mental ability to understand a situation and potential consequences

**dissection**     the act of cutting apart or separating a body to study or examine it

**doctorate**     the highest degree given by a university

**magnetic resonance imaging**     a technique that uses a strong magnetic field to produce computerized images of internal tissues

**motive**     the reason a person does something

**neuroscientist**     a scientist who studies the nervous system, including the brain

**parole**     the supervised release of a prisoner before the end of his sentence

**psychiatrist**     a medical doctor specializing in mental and emotional disorders

**psychologists**     scientists who study mental and emotional processes and behavior

**psychopath**     someone with a personality disorder that results in abnormal social behavior, committed without remorse

| | |
|---|---|
| **subconsciously** | occurring in the subconscious, the part of the mind the person is not aware of |
| **voice stress analysis** | computer software programs designed to pick up changes in voice patterns that indicate stress as a sign that someone may be lying |

# Selected Bibliography

FBI Behavioral Analysis Unit. "Serial Murder: Multi-Disciplinary Perspectives for Investigators." *FBI.gov*. http://www.fbi.gov/stats-services/publications/serial-murder/serial-murder-1.

Gladwell, Malcolm. "Dangerous Minds: Criminal Profiling Made Easy." *New Yorker*, November 12, 2007. http://www.newyorker.com/magazine/2007/11/12/dangerous-minds.

Holmes, Ronald M., and Stephen T. Holmes. *Profiling Violent Crimes: An Investigative Tool*. 4th ed. Los Angeles: Sage, 2009.

McCrary, Gregg O., and Katherine Ramsland. *The Unknown Darkness: Profiling the Predators Among Us*. New York: Morrow, 2003.

Ramsland, Katherine. *Beating the Devil's Game: A History of Forensic Science and Criminal Investigation*. New York: Berkley Books, 2007.

———. *The C.S.I. Effect*. New York: Berkley Boulevard, 2006.

——. *The Human Predator: A Historical Chronicle of Serial Murder and Forensic Investigation*. New York: Berkley Books, 2005.

Ricciuti, Edward. *Science 101: Forensics*. New York: HarperCollins, 2007.

# Websites

### Easy Science for Kids: How to Detect if Someone Is Lying Video

*http://easyscienceforkids.com/how-to-detect-if-someone-is -lying-video-liars-lie-detection-video-for-kids/*

Check out this video to get tips on how to tell if someone is lying to you.

### FFFBI: Perp Walk

*http://www.fffbi.com/games/perp/*

Test your skills of observation and deduction in this game to see if you can identify the perpetrator.

# Index